Genre Fiction

 Essential Question
How can we protect Earth?

Our Beautiful Tree

by Yolanda Garcia
illustrated by George Ulrich

Chapter 1 *Bad News*

"Our treehouse is almost done!" said Jen.

"We just need to finish the ladder!" said Alex.

Jen and Alex were working hard on their treehouse. They couldn't wait to finish it.

"Let's finish tomorrow. I have to do my homework," Alex said.

treehouse

"Jen! Alex! Time to come inside!" their mother called.

"Mom! <u>Check out</u> our treehouse!" Jen said.

"It looks wonderful, kids! But it's getting dark, and you need to finish your homework before dinner!" Mom said.

In Other Words   look at. En español: *mira.*

kitchen

Jen and Alex sat at the dining room table to do their homework. Everybody was busy.

Then Mom said, "Please set the table. It's time for dinner."

At dinner, they talked about <u>their</u> day. Jen said she had done well on her math test. Alex said he had a good soccer practice.

Then Dad said, "We have something to tell you."

Alex and Jen were very curious. What was their father going to say?

| Language Detective | <u>Their</u> is a possessive pronoun. Find another possessive pronoun on page 3. |

dining room

"Our neighbor, Mr. Morris, wants us to cut down our tree," Dad said gently. "The leaves fall into his yard, and he has to rake them. The distance between the tree and his yard is too small."

Jen and Alex just looked at their father. They could not believe what he was saying.

STOP AND CHECK

Why does Mr. Morris want the family to cut down the tree?

6

Chapter 2 *Wonderful Memories*

Everybody was quiet. "No!" said Jen. "We can't cut down the tree! We have our treehouse now!"

"The tree is old and beautiful. It's helping to keep the air clean. It provides shade. Trees are important Earth resources, Dad," said Alex.

window

The whole family had special memories of the tree. They shared their memories.

"I remember when Daddy put up the swing," said Jen. "I rarely played anywhere else that summer!"

"I can't even guess how many times I pushed you in that swing," said Dad.

swing

Every autumn, Jen and Alex liked to jump into enormous piles of leaves.

"Alex, you loved to rake them into a pile and jump right in!" said Mom.

"The leaves always have such beautiful colors," said Alex.

rake

"I remember when we had a picnic for the neighborhood," said Dad. "It was very hot. We <u>couldn't</u> find a cool place to sit. Finally everybody put blankets under the tree branches. It was nice and shady."

Language Detective	<u>Couldn't</u> is a contraction. Find another contraction on page 7.

branch

"This tree has given us so many happy memories," said Mom. "I don't want to cut it down."

"I agree," Alex said.

"We must save our tree!" said Jen.

STOP AND CHECK

What was Jen's special memory of the tree?

11

Chapter 3 *Save Our Tree*

The family sat at the dining room table and discussed the situation.

"Maybe if we talk to Mr. Morris, we can <u>figure this out</u>," said Dad.

"Mr. Morris can be stubborn sometimes," said Mom. "We have to decide what we are going to say."

> **In Other Words** solve the problem. En español: *resolverlo.*

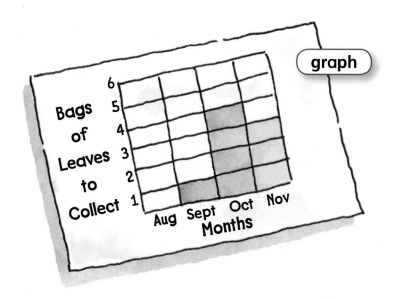

Jen thought they should tell Mr. Morris that trees help keep the air clean.

Then Alex had another idea. "If Mr. Morris is worried about leaves falling in his yard, I can make a graph," he said. "The graph will show when leaves fall. Maybe we can help him rake the leaves!"

Everyone thought giving Mr. Morris a graph was a good idea.

The next day, the whole family went to see Mr. Morris. "Mr. Morris, trees are important," Dad said. "They keep the air clean. They give shade on hot days. And this tree is very special to our family. What if we help rake the leaves? Would you think about keeping the tree?"

Alex showed Mr. Morris his graph. Mr. Morris listened carefully. Then he said, "If the tree is that important to you, and you will help me rake, the tree can stay."

The tree was saved! Everyone came to celebrate. Even Mr. Morris came!

"We saved our beautiful tree!" said Alex proudly.

"I'm so happy!" said Jen.

It was a wonderful day.

STOP AND CHECK

What did Dad say about the tree?

Respond to Reading

Summarize

Use important details to help you summarize *Our Beautiful Tree.*

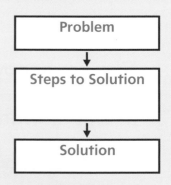

Text Evidence

1. How do you know *Our Beautiful Tree* is fiction? Genre

2. What problem do the characters solve? Problem and Solution

3. Use context clues to figure out the meaning of *our* on page 6. Homophones

4. Write about how the family helped to solve Mr. Morris's problem with the tree. Write About Reading

Compare Texts
Read about the soil in which plants and trees grow.

DIRT!

Soil is more than just dirt. It is one of Earth's most important resources. It has a supply of things people and animals need. Soil is made of little pieces of rock, leaves, and parts of trees. Many insects, like ants, live in the soil. Earthworms do, too.

earthworm

Soil is home to earthworms.

Too much rain, heat, or wind is bad for soil. One way to protect soil is by planting. Plants and grass keep the soil from washing away or getting too hot. Some farmers plant trees near their fields.

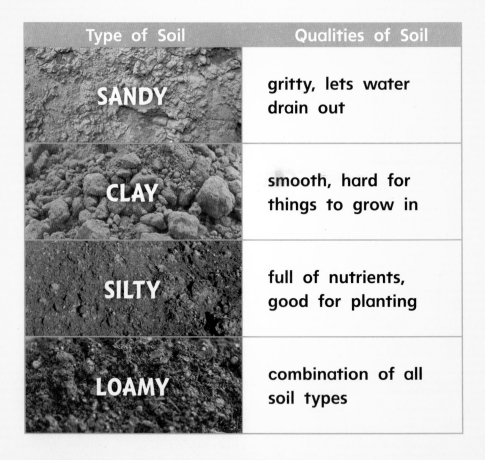

Type of Soil	Qualities of Soil
SANDY	gritty, lets water drain out
CLAY	smooth, hard for things to grow in
SILTY	full of nutrients, good for planting
LOAMY	combination of all soil types

There are many types of soil.

Many foods that you eat come from the soil. Carrots and potatoes grow under the soil. Other vegetables grow on plants in the soil. Fruits do, too. Melons grow on vines that rest on the soil. Dirt is important to everybody!

tomato

Tomatoes need soil to grow, too.

Make Connections

How can we use soil to protect Earth?

Essential Question

Look at both selections. Tell why it is important to protect trees and soil.

Text to Text

Focus on Science

Purpose To find out ways to help the environment

What to Do

Step 1 ▶ Talk with a partner about ways you can help the environment. Think of ways to save energy.

Step 2 ▶ Make a list of the things you can do.

Step 3 ▶ Read over your list. Then use it to make a poster of your favorite ideas.

Conclusion Share your poster with your family. Ask your family to try your ideas.